Transformations

Exploring the Journey of
Infinite Transformations

Maggie Kyle Petraits

BALBOA.
PRESS

A DIVISION OF HAY HOUSE

Balboa Press books may be ordered through booksellers or by contacting:

Balboa Press
A Division of Hay House
1663 Liberty Drive
Bloomington, IN 47403
www.balboapress.com
1 (877) 407-4847

ISBN: 978-1-9822-1135-6 (sc)
ISBN: 978-1-9822-1136-3 (e)

Library of Congress Control Number: 2018910937

Print information available on the last page.

Balboa Press rev. date: 09/24/2018

Inspiration

Through time, the dragonfly has been the symbol of transformation and change. It is considered a powerful totem and spirit that aids in the metamorphosis from water to sky. It represents transformation, spirit connection, growth and change - freedom of mind and spirit and the ability to change quickly.

The dragonfly starts life as a water nymph near the edge of a lake or pond. As it grows and develops wings, it emerges from the water, waiting on rocks nearby for the new wings to dry. Then, with amazing speed and agility (upwards of 45 miles per hour), it takes flight. Seen near these bodies of water, it ferociously feeds on mosquitos. It can fly in six directions, seemingly stopping midair to change direction, skim the water surface, and then flit away in a nanosecond. Dragonflies are fascinating to observe and are blessed companions of nature.

My own journey with this magical creatures began several years ago when doing an extended stay in Indiana. I was recovering from a surgery and a tumultuous divorce. My father was going through cancer treatments and in the quiet afternoons, I found myself sketching and painting, drawing from the nature around me. The dragonfly emerged as a theme. I watched the dragonflies from the bedroom window, fascinated by their flight. They seemed to appear everywhere I went.

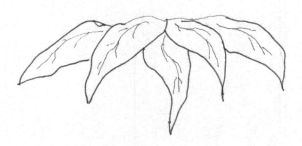

As I healed, I found myself changing, evolving: growing in new thoughts and emotions. During my spiritual awakening, the symbolism of the dragonfly grew with me. As I studied to become an Infinite Possibilities trainer and a Reiki master, the strength of this totem grew stronger, as did my drawings and paintings.

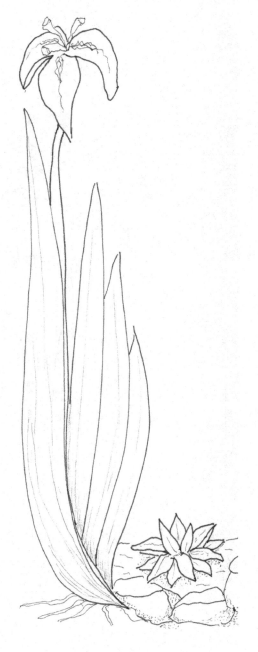

During a women's retreat in Mexico, I had painted dragonflies as gifts. On the evening of the gift exchange, while in a closed conference room, a dragonfly magically and mysteriously appeared. It was my time to share. After sharing the paintings, as I sat down, again the dragonfly appeared, this time landing on my outstretched hand.

In many of the drawings, the iris appears alongside my dragonflies. Irises also have a wonderful symbolism dating back to the Greek Goddess Iris. Rainbows, transitions, faith, hope, courage and wisdom are all associated with the beautiful flower.

This Coloring Book is filled with pen-and-ink drawings of these mystical, magical creatures as they appear to me . They represent a metamorphic growth in my art. Many of these have appeared during meditations, dreams or even Reiki healings.

Let the dragonfly's spirit guide you as you whimsically color its wings with your interpretation.

Enlightenment

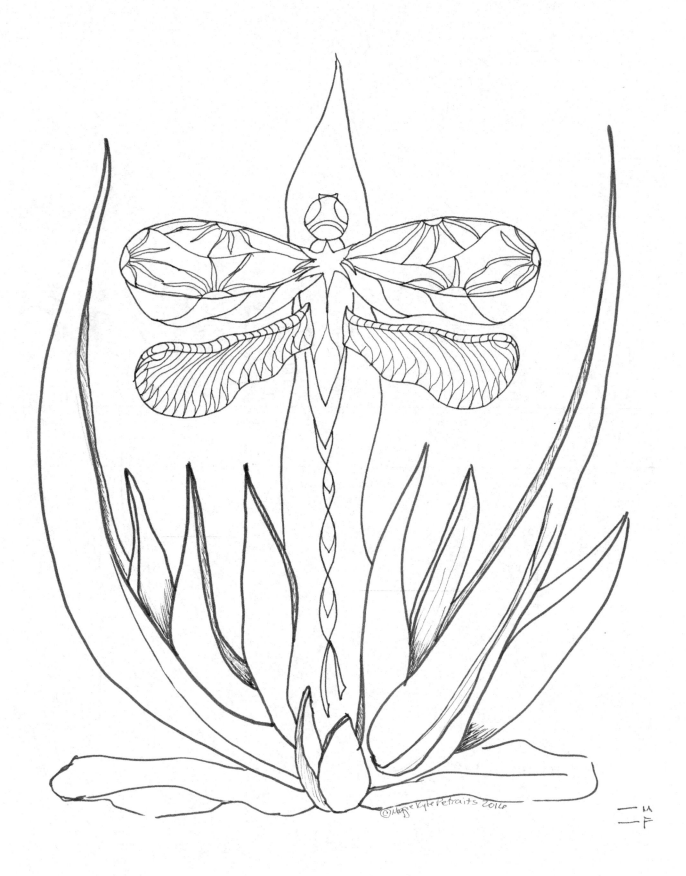

©Maggie Kyle Portraits 2016

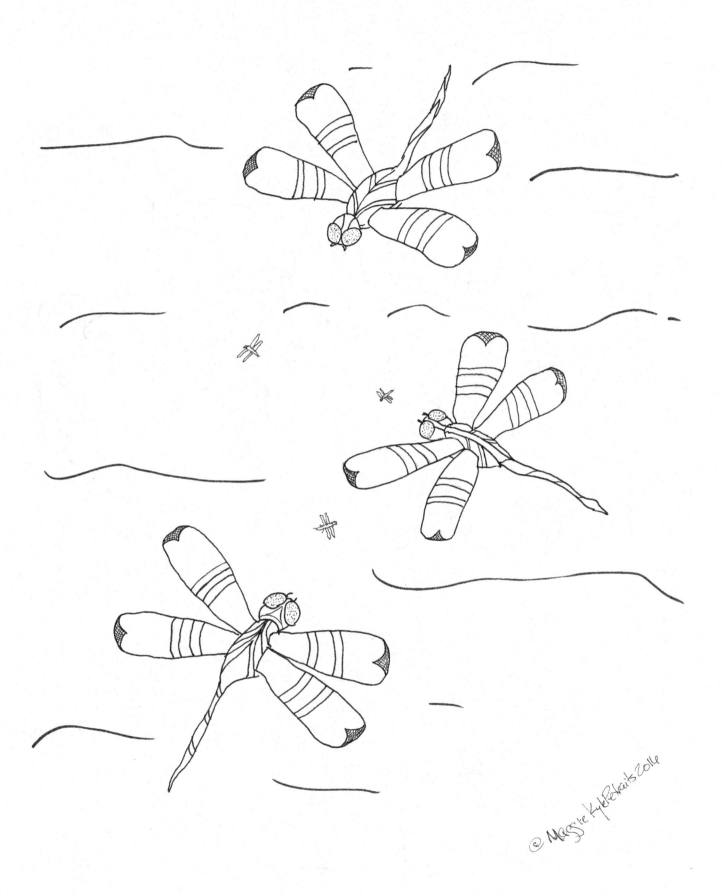

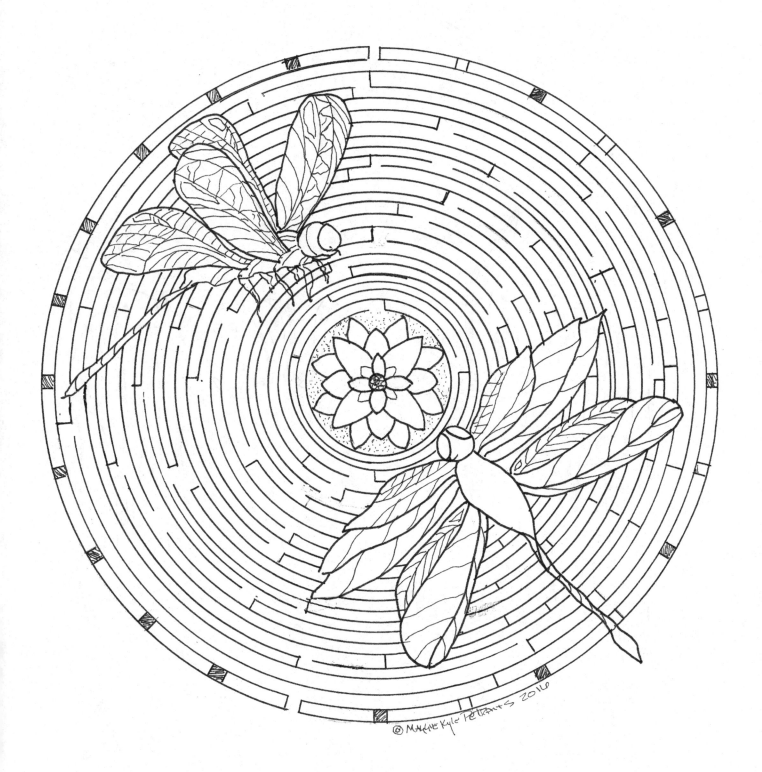

© Mattie Kyle Petrants 2016

©Maggie Kyte Portraits 2016

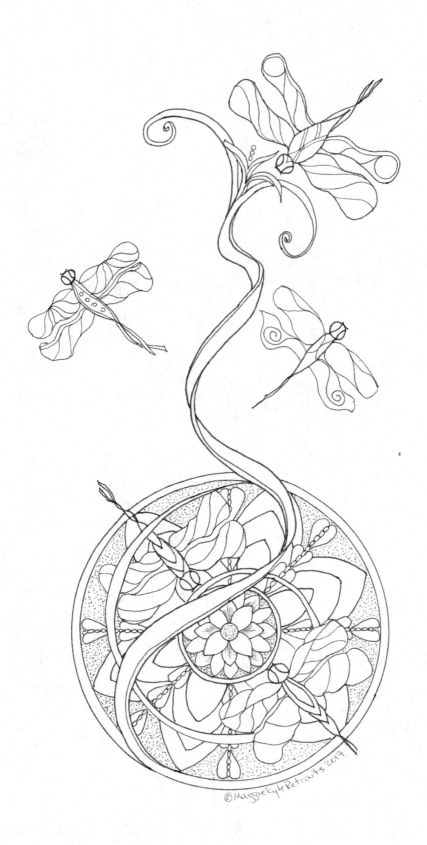

©MaggieKyleRetreats 2017

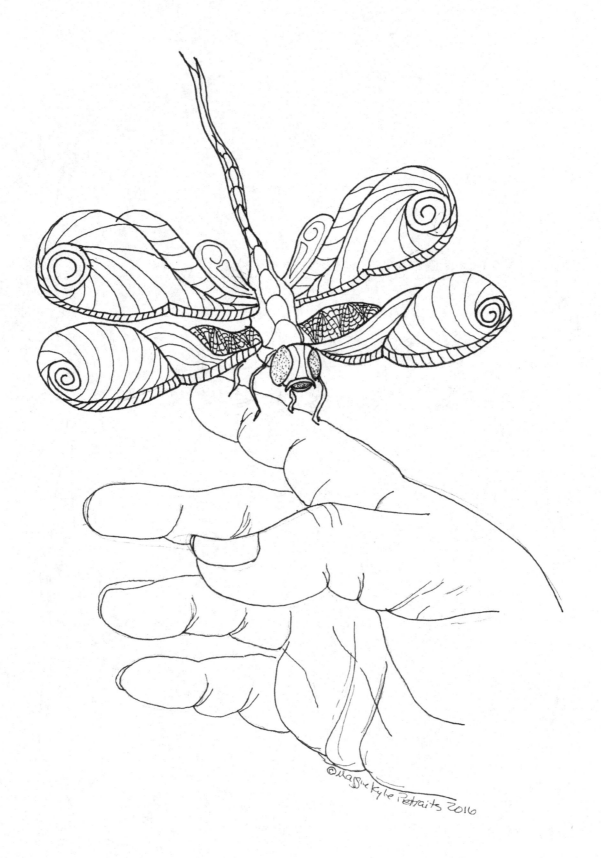

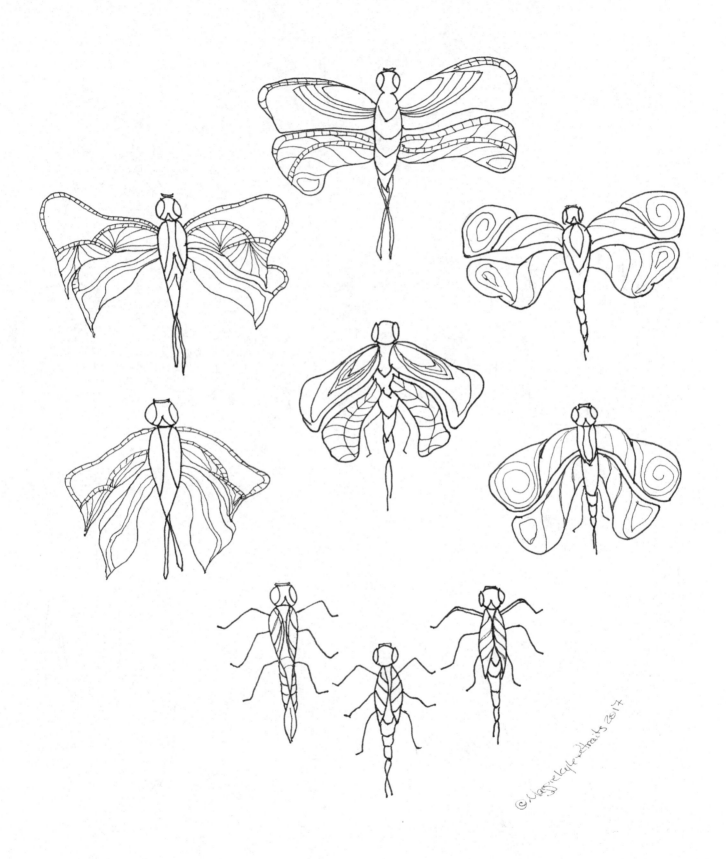

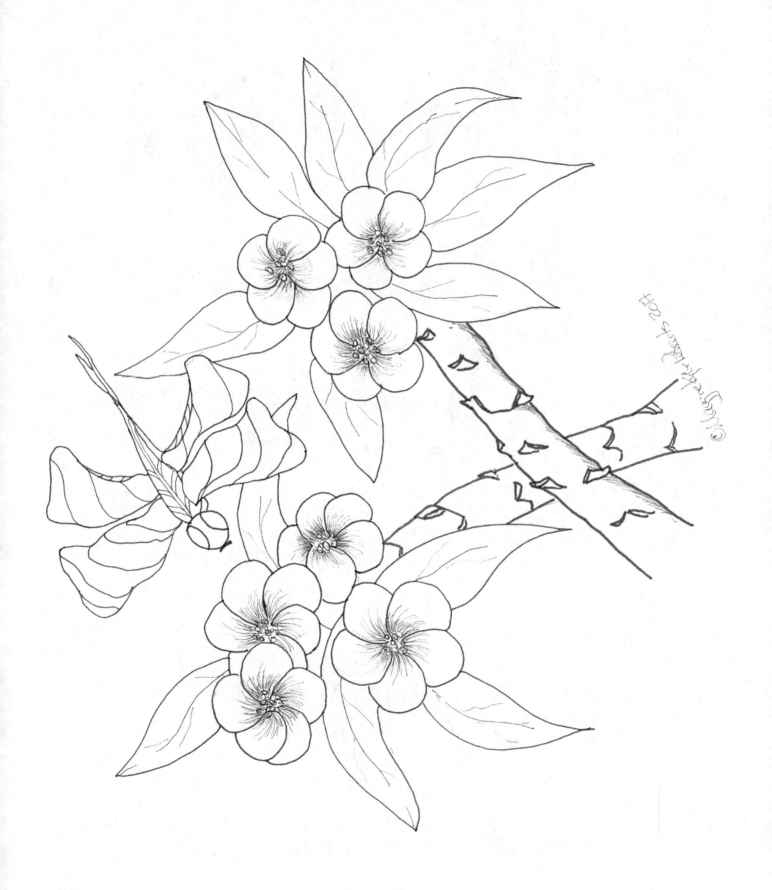

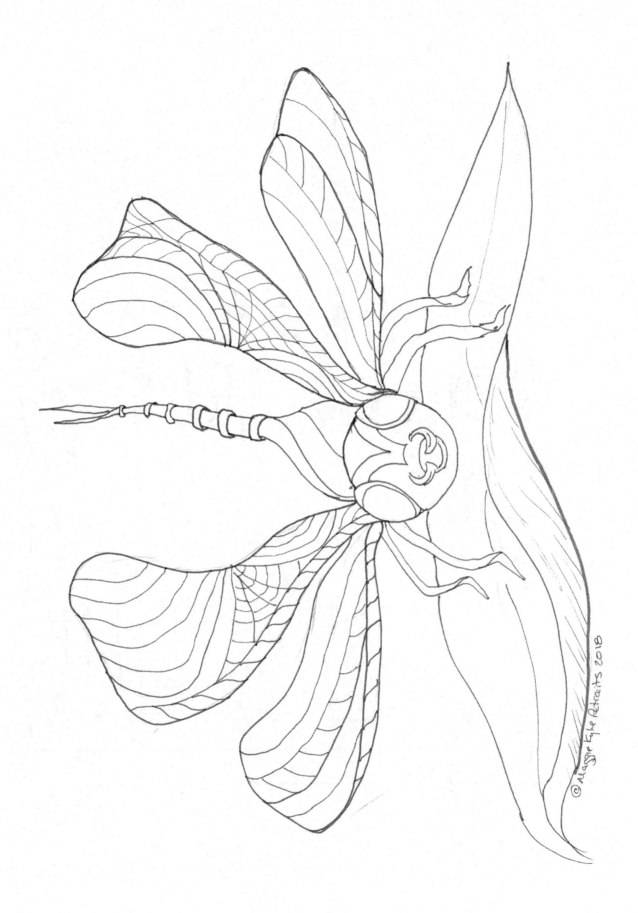

With Gratitude.

I begin each day with gratitude - to those who have impacted my life in the past 24 hours, for victories large and small, for lessons learned, for my art, inspiration, family, friends. This coloring book was born of gratitude.

When I first discovered Mike Dooley's writings and the TUT website, I remember thinking "I'm not the only one who thinks this way!". It was a relief. I went on to become an Infinite Possibilities trainer - which led me to meet so many of the people who influenced this coloring book. Thank you to Darlene for slipping a little piece of paper in my hand that said go sign up for your Notes from the Universe.

To Regena Garrepy and your Red Hot Visionista program, you helped me acknowledge and step into my power as an artist. For Leigh Daniels and Jonathon Benjamin creating the Possibilities in Paradise (PIP) retreat, for this is truly where this coloring book was conceived - in a dream on the last night of the retreat. After searching all over Key West for a coloring book with my beloved dragonflies... and not finding one. For Ashley, Sara Ann and Anella encouraging me when I shared my vision. And to Gary for asking me to paint a dragonfly for his heart.

The past year, in Joanna Lindenbaum's Sacred Depths coaching program, has greatly influenced several drawings. Reflection in particular came to me during one of our classes. I don't think I took too many notes that day but had great sketches! For my coaching buddy Monisha as she listened to my ideas and shared my enthusiasm.

My dear friend Meg who encouraged me when I felt overwhelmed and who helped me put Mystery on paper. As we talked, I sketched. To Tina Marie who helped me find one of my guides, the one who appears here. She came to me in a meditation, asking to be personified. My Reiki group of SW Florida and the ABWA Imperial River sisters have waited with baited breath for this book to be born. To Jean, Mama Badger, Neil, and all of my friends who have watched me draw. Ta Da!!! Here it is!

To my sister who saw the drawings and acknowledged me. Her support and encouragement mean the world to me

Inspire really happened. Bliss came to me in the depths of grief. Enlightenment was the first drawing. Pursuit was for the young boy who was afraid of dragonflies until he understood their purpose. Each drawing has a story, symbolism and meaning. Two years of drawings, emotions and inspiration are represented here.

And I must also give gratitude for my parents. They encouraged us siblings to march to the beat of a different drummer, to find our creative outlet. Their love and support has carried me through so much. I know dad is looking over my shoulder with love from above. Mom may think I'm a little crazy but she has always encouraged me to follow my dreams.

I choose the thoughts and dreams that I believe are part of my journey, the infinite possibilities that are within each of us. Thank you for choosing to be a part of this journey.

Happy Coloring!

Maggie Kyle Petraits

Printed in the United States
By Bookmasters